VAN GOGH
BY

Vincent

Irises, 1889, J. Paul Getty Museum, Malibu, California

VAN GOGH
BY

Vincent

ARTISTS BY THEMSELVES
EDITED BY RACHEL BARNES

ALFRED A. KNOPF
NEW YORK
1990

This is a Borzoi Book
Published by Alfred A. Knopf, Inc.

Introduction Text Copyright © 1990 by Rachel Barnes

Published in the United States by Alfred A. Knopf, Inc.
Distributed by Random House, Inc., New York.

Originally published in Great Britain by
Webb & Bower (Publishers) Limited, Exeter, Devon

Series devised by Nicky Bird

Designed by Vic Giolitto

Library of Congress Cataloging-in-Publication Data
Barnes, Rachel.
    Artists by themselves. Van Gogh/Rachel Barnes. — 1st American ed.
      p. cm.
    "Originally published in Great Britain by Webb & Bower
(Publishers) Limited, Exeter"—T.p. verso.
    ISBN 0–394–58909–2 : $16.95
    1. Gogh, Vincent van. 1853–1890 — Sources. 2. Painting — Themes.
motives. I. Title.
ND653.G7B33 1990
759.9492 — dc20   90–52733
                                      CIP

Manufactured in Italy
First American Edition

CONTENTS

Introduction 6

Van Gogh by Vincent 18

Chronology 78

Acknowledgements 80

INTRODUCTION

Well, the truth is, we can only make our pictures speak. But yet, my dear brother, there is that I have always told you, and I repeat it once more with all the earnestness that can be expressed by the effort of a mind diligently fixed on trying to do as well as possible – I tell you again that I shall always consider you to be something more than a simple dealer in Corots, that through my meditation you have your part in the actual production of some canvases which will retain their calm even in the catastrophe.

These words were found scribbled on a piece of paper in Vincent van Gogh's pocket on the day he shot himself, 29 July 1890, at the age of thirty-seven. It was to be his last letter to his brother Theo, the last in a seventeen-year-old, almost daily correspondence and, as it transpired, since he died two days later, Vincent's last attempt to thank Theo for all he had done to help him as a brother, friend and patron. For without Theo's extraordinary concern, demonstrated by his practical advice, financial help and tireless emotional support, it is doubtful whether Vincent would have lived even as long as he did. His painting career was one of the shortest and most intense in the history of Western art – in ten years, 1880-1890, he progressed from stumbling, uncertain beginnings in Etten to the sun-drenched vision of Arles.

No-one understood the debt he owed his brother more than Vincent himself, as this last letter shows. In an earlier letter he had written: 'I will give you back the money or give away my soul.' Their empathy and love for each other is apparent throughout their

Two Self Portraits, 1887, Vincent van Gogh Foundation/National Museum
Vincent van Gogh, Amsterdam

Birchwood with a Flock of Sheep, Vincent van Gogh Foundation/National Museum Vincent van Gogh, Amsterdam

correspondence, giving the reader an insight into Vincent's troubled and anxious personality, and showing his daily thoughts and preoccupations about his great vocation – his painting.

Vincent van Gogh was born in Groot-Zundert in Holland in 1853. He was named after his brother, who was born exactly a year before him but had died after a few months, and the boy consequently suffered from the feeling that he was a replacement for someone else. His was not a happy childhood. His diffident, highly strung and over-sensitive temperament isolated him from his schoolmates, as it was to all his life. His one great ally from earliest days was Theo, and as teenagers they made a pact, swearing never to desert each other.

The Sheafbinder, Vincent van Gogh Foundation/National Museum Vincent van Gogh, Amsterdam

Vincent was first employed by his Uncle's art business, Goupil and Co, and he worked for them in The Hague, London and Paris. In London he frequented the National Gallery and, also important for his future work, became an admirer of Dickens. But Vincent's imaginative and volatile personality could hardly have been less suited to business and he soon left, deciding to devote himself entirely to God, preaching in the poor mining villages of the Borinage.

Like everything else Vincent did in his life, he put his heart and soul into helping the poor, nursing the sick and going down into the most dangerous mines to preach. Sadly, his eccentric manner, his impassioned speeches, and his extreme commitment – he gave away his food, his clothes and his money – had the effect of frightening his would-be converts, and after a while he had to admit defeat. He knew he had a vocation, but he had not as yet found it. 'There is something within me, what is it then?' he wrote to Theo, 'How can I make myself useful and what end can I serve?'

Vincent was twenty-seven, with ten years of his life left to live, when he finally realized that he wanted to be a painter. 'I cannot tell you how happy I am to have taken up drawing again. I have been thinking of it, but I always considered the thing impossible and beyond my reach,' he wrote to Theo. In these early years Vincent travelled a good deal, spending time in Brussels, Etten, The Hague, Drenthe, Neunen and Antwerp. His early canvases – his Dutch period – employ a dark, sombre palette, influenced by Rembrandt in their use of chiaroscuro. From the start he had decided ideas on the emotional value of his work. He wrote to Theo from The Hague:

> I want you to understand clearly my conception of art . . .
> What I want and aim at is confoundedly difficult, and yet I do

Old Vineyard with Peasant Woman, 1890, Vincent van Gogh Foundation/National Museum Vincent van Gogh, Amsterdam

not think I aim too high. I want to do drawings which *touch* some people ... In either figure or landscape I should wish to express, not sentimental melancholy, but serious sorrow ... I want to progress so far that people will say of my work, he feels deeply, he feels tenderly – notwithstanding my so-called roughness, perhaps even because of it ... what am I in most people's eyes? A nonentity, or an eccentric and disagreeable man – somebody who has no position in society and never will have, in short, the lowest of the low. Very well ... then I should want my work to show what is in the heart of such an eccentric, of such a nobody. This is my ambition, which is, in spite of everything, founded less on anger than on love.

He struggled hard in those early years and experienced many technical difficulties in trying to find a style which could express what was in the 'heart of such a nobody'. Often his letters to Theo at this time give way to despair and loneliness. His dedication to his art was absolute and, with uncanny prescience, he predicted that he only had a few years left in which to fulfil his aim.

> I do *not* intend to spare myself, nor to avoid emotions or difficulties – I don't care much whether I live a longer or shorter time ... The world concerns me only insofar as I feel a certain indebtedness and duty toward it because I have walked this earth for thirty years, and, out of gratitude, want to leave some souvenir in the shape of drawings or pictures – not made to please a certain taste in art, but to express a sincere human feeling.

Finally, he accepted Theo's offer to come and stay with him in Paris, where the latter had set up as an art dealer. Theo wanted him to meet the Impressionists, and was anxious for his brother to have the stimulation of conversing with fellow artists.

For a while Vincent was happier in Paris – under the influence of Impressionism and a warmer climate his palette brightened considerably, and he began to experiment with the pointillist technique. He wrote back to his family:

> The air of France clarifies one's ideas and does one good, much good, the world of good. I don't know what impression Paris might make on you. The first time I saw it it was mostly the sad things about it that I felt ... And this is how I felt for

Young Peasant with a Sickle, 1881, Rijksmuseum Kröller-Müller, Otterlo, The Netherlands

a long time, though later I realized that Paris is a hot bed of ideas, and that people are trying to get out of life everything it is possible to get out of it.

Whilst he was staying in Paris, Vincent also began to be increasingly impressed by the Japanese prints which had been influencing the more experimental painters since their importation into Paris in the 1850s. When he made the decision to leave Paris for the South of France, he told Theo that he intended to 'create his own Japan' there and paint like a Japanese artist. Later he wrote to Gauguin, recalling his arrival in Arles by train in the February of

1888, 'There is still present in my mind the emotion produced by my own journey from Paris to Arles last winter. How I peered out to see whether it was like Japan yet! Childish, wasn't it?'

It was during this final period in Arles – the last two years of his life – that Vincent achieved his mature style, producing canvas after canvas in a frenzy of work or 'a rage of work', as he called it to Theo. It was a time fraught with personal difficulties; his dream of establishing a colony of artists in the South of France was shattered after the visit of the first painter. Gauguin's turbulent three-month stay ended with Vincent's first severe breakdown and his attack upon himself – the cutting of his ear which led to his first visit to St Rémy Mental Hospital. It was to be the first of a number of such visits as his attacks became increasingly frequent.

Vincent lived a life of almost unrelieved isolation and loneliness, increasingly so as his mental illness cut him off from the people around him. Left alone with his thoughts and his feelings, many of which terrified and overwhelmed him, Theo became a lifeline: the only person in whom he could confide without fear of rebuff or misunderstanding.

Vincent poured out all his thoughts in his letters, from the smaller details of everyday life to his more profound thoughts on the nature of existence, and in particular his fears for his own life. More importantly for the selection of paintings in this book, Vincent also expressed in great detail his thoughts about his art. Using sketches and descriptions, he kept Theo informed of the majority of the paintings he was working on. As a result, we are left with some of the best and most detailed documentation of an artist's *oeuvre* in the history of European painting. For this reason it is especially fascinating and illuminating to see Vincent's words to Theo juxtaposed with the specific works he had in mind.

Theo was by no means Vincent's only correspondent, however.

The Café Terrace at Arles at Night, 1888, Rijksmuseum, Kröller-Müller, Otterlo, The Netherlands

The Sower, 1888, Vincent van Gogh Foundation/National Museum Vincent van Gogh, Amsterdam

Alongside the thirty paintings in this book, which represent his ten active years as a painter, there are quotations from letters to his mother, to his sister Wilhelmina, to fellow painters – Gauguin, Bernard and Albert Aurier – and to Theo's wife Johanna. But by far the majority, and most revealing, are those to Theo. He alone understood Vincent's passionate love of his art, his impossible temperament, and his ultimate inability to cope with his illness and loneliness. 'La tristesse durera', 'The sadness will never go away', were Vincent's last words to his brother as he died in his arms. Theo understood even this final despair: temperamentally so close to Vincent, it was a despair he knew only too well.

The strain of those ten years of intense creativity, and his close involvement with his brother's decline, broke Theo just as it had broken Vincent. He died only six months after Vincent's suicide: the two brothers were buried side by side in the church yard of Auvers-sur-Oise.

Despite all his efforts, during Vincent's lifetime Theo had succeeded in selling only one painting by his brother. He died leaving only his wife Johanna and his baby son to see Vincent's name established as one of the greatest in nineteenth-century European painting. Prophetically, Vincent had written to Theo at the very start of his vocation to paint: 'I feel within me a power that I must develop, a fire not to put out but fanned into flame, although I don't know what it will lead to and shouldn't be surprised if it was something grim.'

Self Portrait with Grey Felt Hat
1887

Vincent van Gogh Foundation
National Museum Vincent van Gogh, Amsterdam

Now I must bore you with certain abstract things, but I hope you will listen to them patiently. I am a man of passions, capable of and subject to doing more or less foolish things, which I happen to repent, more or less, afterwards. Now and then I speak and act too hastily, when it would have been better to wait patiently. I think other people sometimes make the same mistakes. Well, this being the case, what's to be done? Must I consider myself a dangerous man, incapable of anything? I don't think so. But the problem is to try every means to put those selfsame passions to good use. For instance, to name one of the passions, I have a more or less irresistible passion for books, and I continually want to instruct myself, to study if you like, just as much as I want to eat my bread. You certainly will be able to understand this. When I was in other surroundings, in the surroundings of pictures and works of art, you know how I had a violent passion for them, reaching the highest pitch of enthusiasm. And I am not sorry about it, for even now, far from the land, I am often homesick for the land of pictures.

Letter to Theo, 1883

Sorrow

Lithograph, November 1882

Vincent van Gogh Foundation
National Museum Vincent van Gogh, Amsterdam

... Last winter I met a pregnant woman, deserted by the man whose child she carried.

A pregnant woman who had to walk the streets in winter, had to earn her bread, you understand how.

I took this woman for a model, and have worked with her all winter. I could not pay her the full wages of a model, but that did not prevent my paying her rent, and thank God, so far I have been able to protect her and her child from hunger and cold by sharing my own bread with her.

When I met this woman, she attracted my attention because she looked ill. I made her take baths and as much nourishing food as I could afford, and she has become much stronger ...

Letter to Theo, 1882

I have to put up with the gossip, because I am constantly in her company, but why should that worry me? I have never received such support as from this ugly?? and blemished woman. To me she is beautiful, and I find her exactly what I need. Life has flowed over her body and sorrow and experience have left their mark. At the moment I can gain something from that.

Letter to Van Reppard, 1882

Sorrow

Mother and Child
1881-3

Vincent van Gogh Foundation
National Museum Vincent van Gogh, Amsterdam

I want to do drawings which touch some people ... in short I want
to progress so far that they will say of my work: He feels deeply, he
feels tenderly – notwithstanding my so-called roughness, or perhaps
even because of it.

Letter to Theo, The Hague, 1883

The Loom
May 1884

Christie's, London

I have a strong fellow-feeling for them (miners and weavers) and I'd count myself lucky if one day I could draw them in such a way that these new or virtually new types could be seen by the public ... The man in the abyss, de profundis, is the miner; the other one, who looks like a dreamer, a thinker, a somnambulist even, that is the weaver.

Letter to Theo, 1884

The Potato Eaters
April-May 1885

Vincent van Gogh Foundation
National Museum Vincent van Gogh, Amsterdam

What I have tried hard to convey is the sense that these people sitting in the lamplight, picking up their potatoes from the dish and eating them with their hands, have actually worked the land, so that my picture gives dignity to manual labour and to the food they have won for themselves by honest toil. I've tried to make it expressive of a way of life quite different from that of cultivated people like ourselves. So I don't at all expect people to like it ...

Letter to Theo, 1885

Worn Out: At Eternity's Gate
Reworked May 1890

Collection: State Museum Kröller-Müller, Otterlo, The Netherlands

It seems to me it's a painter's duty to try to put an idea into his work
... I have tried to express (but I cannot do it well or so strikingly as
it is in reality; this is merely a weak reflection in a dark mirror)
what seems to me one of the strongest proofs of the existence of
'quelque chose là-haute' in which Millet believed namely the
existence of God and eternity – certainly in the infinitely touching
expression of such a little old man, which he himself is perhaps
unconscious of, when he is sitting quietly in his corner by the fire.
At the same time there is something noble, something great, which
cannot be destined for the worms; Israels has painted it so
beautifully ...

Letter to Theo, The Hague, 1882

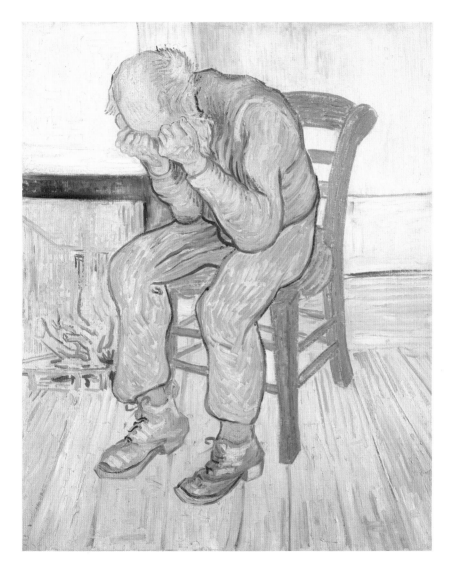

Portrait of Père Tanguy
1887

Musée Rodin, Paris

I was sorry afterward not to have asked old Tanguy for the paints all the same, not that there would be the least advantage in doing so – on the contrary – but he's such a funny old soul, and I still think of him many a time. Don't forget to say hello for me if you see him, and tell him that if he wants pictures for his window, he can have some from here, and the best at that. Oh! it seems to me more and more that *people* are the root of everything, and though it will always be a melancholy thought that you yourself are not in real life, I mean, that it's more worthwhile to work in flesh and blood itself than in paint or plaster, more worthwhile to make children than pictures or carry on business, all the same you feel that you're alive when you remember that you have friends who are outside real life as much as you.

But just because it's what people have in their hearts that matters, and it is at the heart of all business dealings too, we must make friendships in Holland, or rather revive them. More especially since, as far as the Impressionist cause is concerned, there is little fear now that we shall not win.

Letter to Theo, Arles, 1888

Souvenir de Mauve
1888

Rijksmuseum, Kröller-Müller, Otterlo, The Netherlands

... I have been working on a size 20 canvas in the open air in an orchard, lilac ploughland, a reed fence, two pink peach trees against a sky of glorious blue and white. Probably the best landscape I have done. I had just brought it home when I received from our sister a Dutch notice in memory of Mauve, with his portrait (the portrait, very good), the text, poor and nothing in it, a pretty water colour. Something – I don't know what – took hold of me and brought a lump to my throat, and I wrote on my picture.

Souvenir de Mauve

Vincent Theo

and if you agree we two will send it, such as it is, to Mrs Mauve. I chose the best study I've painted here purposely; I don't know what they'll say about it at home, but that does not matter to us; it seemed to me that everything in memory of Mauve must be at once tender and very gay, and not a study in any graver key ...

Letter to Theo, Arles, 1888

The Postman Roulin
February-March 1888

Rijksmuseum, Kröller-Müller, Otterlo, The Netherlands

A socratic type, no less socratic for being a bit of an alcoholic, and consequently of a high colour. His wife had just given birth, the good man glowed with satisfaction. He's an awful old republican, like Père Tanguy ... He held himself too stiffly when he posed, which is why I painted him twice, the second time in a single sitting.

Letter to Emile Bernard, Arles, 1888

The Drawbridge
April 1888

Rijkmuseum, Kröller-Müller, Otterlo, The Netherlands

As for work, I've come back today with a size 15 canvas; it's a drawbridge with a little cart going across it, standing out against the blue sky – the river is blue too, the banks orange-coloured and grassy, and there's a group of washerwomen in traditional jackets and caps of various colours.

Letter to Theo, Arles, 1888

The Yellow House, Arles
June 1888

Vincent van Gogh Foundation
National Museum Vincent van Gogh, Amsterdam

– I live in a little yellow house with a green door and green blinds, whitewashed inside – on the white walls very brightly coloured Japanese prints, red tiles on the floor – the house in the full sunlight – over it an intensely blue sky, and the shadows in the middle of the day much shorter than in our country. Well – can you understand that one may be able to paint something like this with only a few strokes of the brush? . . .

Letter to Wilhelmina, Arles, 1888

Boats on the Beach at Saintes-Maries-de-la-Mer
June 1888

Vincent van Gogh Foundation
National Museum Vincent van Gogh, Amsterdam

– What strikes me here, and what makes painting so attractive is the clearness of the air . . .

. . . I don't need Japanese pictures here, for I am always telling myself that *here I am in Japan* which means that I have only to open my eyes and paint what is right in front of me.

. . . I wish you could spend some time here, you would feel it after a while, one's sight changes: you see things with an eye more Japanese, you feel colour differently. The Japanese draw quickly, very quickly, like a lightning flash, because their nerves are finer, their feelings simpler.

I am convinced that I shall set my individuality free simply by staying on here.

I have only been here a few months, but tell me this – could I, in Paris, have done the drawing of the boats in an hour? Even without the respective frame, I do it now without measuring, just by letting my pen go . . .

Letter to Wilhelmina, 1888

The Zoave

1888

What impassions me most – much, much more than all the rest of my metier – is the portrait, the modern portrait. I seek it in colour, and surely I am not the only one to seek it in this direction. I *should like* – mind you, far be it from me to say that I shall be able to do it, although this is what I am aiming at – I *should like* to paint portraits which would appear after a century to the people living then as apparitions. By which I mean that I do not endeavour to achieve this by a photographic resemblance, but by means of our impassioned expressions – that is to say, using our knowledge of and our modern taste for colour as a means of arriving at the expression and the intensification of the character.

Letter to Theo, Arles, 1888

Sunflowers

August 1888

Vincent van Gogh Foundation
National Museum Vincent van Gogh, Amsterdam

I'm painting with all the gusto of a Marseillais eating bouillabaisse, which won't come as any surprise to you when you learn that what I'm painting are some big sunflowers ... I work on them every morning starting at sunrise as they are flowers that wilt quickly and you need to do the whole thing in one go.

Letter to Theo, Arles, 1888

La Mousmé

1888

National Gallery of Art, Washington DC

Oh, my dear brother, sometimes I know so well what I want. I can very well do without God both in my life and in my painting, but I cannot, ill as I am, do without something which is greater than I, which is my life – the power to create.

And if, frustrated in the physical power, a man tries to create thoughts instead of children, he is still part of humanity.

And in a picture I want to say something comforting, as music is comforting. I want to paint men and women with that something of the eternal which the halo used to symbolize, and which we seek to convey by the actual radiance and vibration of our colouring.

Portraiture so understood does not become like an Ary Scheffer just because there is a blue sky in the background, as in 'St Augustine.' For Ary Scheffer is so little of a colourist.

Letter to Theo, Arles, 1888

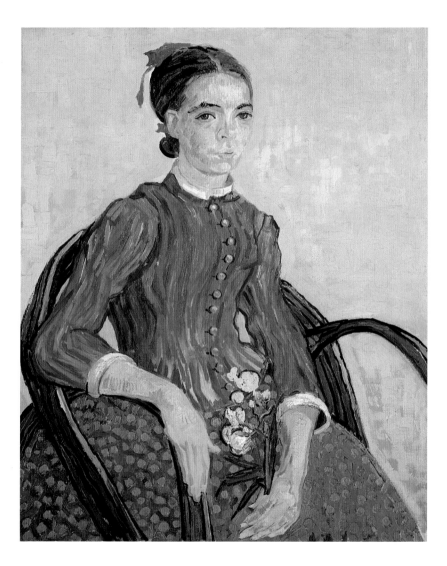

Night Café
September 1888

Yale University Art Gallery, New Haven

In my painting of the Night Café I've tried to show how the café is a place where you can face ruin or become mad or commit crimes. What I've tried to do is use contrasts of delicate pink with blood red and winy purple, soft Louis XV and Veronese greens in contrast with yellowy-greens and hard blue-greens, all in the pallid sulphurous glow of a furnace in hell, expressing something of the powers of darkness of a low dive. All nonetheless with an appearance of Japanese gaiety and the good spirits of Tartarin himself.

Letter to Theo, Arles, 1888

Van Gogh's Bedroom at Arles (Detail)
October 1888

Vincent van Gogh Foundation
National Museum Vincent van Gogh, Amsterdam

A size 30 canvas of my bedroom with the white wood furniture you remember. Well, I've enormously enjoyed doing this bare interior, which is of a Seurat-like simplicity: flat colours, but coarsely applied in a thick impasto, the walls pale lilac, the floor of streaked and faded red, chairs and bed in chrome yellow, pillows and sheet a very pale greeny lemon, the coverlet blood red, the wash-stand an orangey colour, the basin blue and window green.

You see, I wanted to express absolute repose, through using all these different tones, the only white being the little note of the mirror in a black frame (which makes us a fourth pair of complementary colours in it).

Letter to Gauguin, Arles, 1888

L'Arlésienne
1888

Musée d'Orsay, Paris

. . . Thank you for having written to me again, old fellow, and rest
assured that since my return I have thought of you every day. I
stayed in Paris only three days, and the noise, etc, of Paris had such
a bad effect on me that I thought it wise for my head's sake to fly to
the country; but for that, I should soon have dropped in on you.
And it gives me enormous pleasure when you say the Arlésienne's
portrait, which was based strictly on your drawing, is to your
liking. I tried to be religiously faithful to your drawing, while
nevertheless taking the liberty of interpreting through the medium
of colour the sober character and the style of the drawing in
question. It is a synthesis of the Arlésiennes, if you like; as syntheses
of the Arlésiennes are rare, take this as a work belonging to you and
me as a summary of our months of work together. For my part I
paid for doing it with another month of illness, but I also know that
it is a canvas which will be understood by you, and by a very few
others, as we would wish it to be understood. My friend Dr Gachet
here has taken to it altogether after two or three hesitations, and
says, 'How difficult it is to be simple' . . .

Letter to Gauguin, Auvers, 1890

La Berceuse (Madame Roulin)
December 1888-March 1889

Vincent van Gogh Foundation
National Museum Vincent van Gogh, Amsterdam

... What you say about 'La Berceuse' pleases me, it is very true that the common people, who are content with chromos (popular coloured prints) and melt when they hear a barrel organ, are in some vague way right, perhaps more sincere than certain men about town who go to the Salon ...

Letter to Theo, St Rémy, June 1889

Starry Night
June 1889

Musée d'Orsay, Paris

That raises again the eternal question: is the whole of life visible to us, or do we in fact know only the one hemisphere before we die? For my part I know nothing with any certainty, but the sight of the stars makes me dream, in the same simple way as I dream about the black dots representing towns and villages on a map. Why I ask myself, should the shining dots in the sky be any less accessible to us than the black dots on the map of France? If we take the train to get to Tarascon or Rouen, then we take death to go to a star. What is certainly true in this reasoning is that while we are alive we cannot go to a star, any more than, once dead, we could catch a train. It seems not impossible to me that cholera, gravel, phthisis and cancer could be the means of celestial transportation, just as steam-boats, omnibuses and railways serve that function on earth. To die peacefully of old age would be to go there on foot.

Letter to Theo, 1889

Self Portrait with Palette

September 1889

From the Collection of Mrs John Hay Whitney, New York

It is said – and I can easily believe it – that it's difficult to know oneself, but nor is it easy to paint oneself. So I'm working on two self-portraits at the moment – lacking any other model – for it's more than time I did some figure work. One, I started the first day I got up, I was thin and pale as the devil. It's a dark blue-mauve with the head whitish and the hair yellow, a colour study therefore ...

Letter to Theo, 1889

[59]

Olive Field
1889

Rijksmuseum, Kröller-Müller, Otterlo, The Netherlands

Well, probably the day is not far off when they will paint olive trees in all kinds of ways, just as they paint the Dutch willows and pollard willows, just as they painted the Norman apple tree ever since Daubigny and Cesar de Cock. The effect of daylight, of the sky, makes it possible to extract an infinity of subjects from the olive tree. Now, I on my part sought contrasting effects in the foliage, changing with the hues of the sky. At times the whole is a pure all-pervading blue, namely when the tree bears its pale flowers, and big blue flies, emerald rose beetles and cicadas in great numbers are hovering around it. Then, as the bronzed leaves are getting riper in tone, the sky is brilliant and radiant with green and orange, or, more often even, in autumn, when the leaves acquire something of the violet things of the ripe fig, the violet effect will manifest itself vividly through the contrasts, with the large sun taking on a white tint within a halo of clear and pale citron yellow. At times, after a shower, I have also seen the whole sky coloured pink and bright orange, which gave an exquisite value and colouring to the silvery grey-green. And in the midst of that there were women, likewise pink, gathering fruits.

Letter to J. J. Isaacson, 1889

Meadow with Cypress Trees
1890

National Gallery, London

Cypresses for you, if you will do me the favour of accepting it in remembrance of your article. I am still working on it at the moment, as I want to put in a little figure. The cypress is so characteristic of the scenery of Provence; you will feel it and say: 'Even the colour is black'. Until now I have not been able to do them as I feel them; the emotions that grip me in front of nature can cause me to lose consciousness, and then follows a fortnight during which I cannot work. Nevertheless, before leaving here I feel sure I shall return to the charge and attack the cypresses. The study I have set aside for you represents a group of them in the corner of a wheat field during a summer mistral. So it is a note of a certain nameless black in the restless gusty blue of the wide sky, and the vermilion of the poppies contrasting with this dark note.

Letter to Albert Aurier, 1890

Irises (Detail)
May 1890

Vincent van Gogh Foundation
National Museum Vincent van Gogh, Amsterdam

I'm working at the moment on a canvas of roses against a light green background and two canvases of big bunches of mauve irises, one against a pink background, in which the combination of greens, pinks and mauves gives a soft and harmonious effect. In contrast, the other bunch of mauve flowers (ranging from carmine and pure Prussian blue) stands out sharply against a brilliant lemon yellow ground, with other tones of yellow in the vase and the base.

Letter to Theo, 1890

[65]

Road with Cypress and a Star
1890

Rijksmuseum, Kröller-Müller, Otterlo, The Netherlands

. . . The cypresses are always occupying my thoughts, I should like to make something of them like the canvases of the sunflowers, because it astonishes me that they have not yet been done as I see them.

It is as beautiful of line and proportion as an Egyptian obelisk.

And the green has a quality of such distinction.

It is a splash of black in a sunny landscape, but it is one of the most interesting black notes, and the most difficult to hit off exactly that I can imagine . . .

Letter to Theo, St Rémy, June 1889

Dr Gachet
1890

Musée d'Orsay, Paris

... I painted a portrait of Dr Gachet with an expression of melancholy, which would seem to look like a grimace to many who saw the canvas. And yet it is necessary to paint it like this, for otherwise one could not get an idea of the extent to which, in comparison with the old portraits, there is expression in our modern heads, and passion – like a waiting for things as well as a growth. Sad and yet gentle, but clear and intelligent – this is how one ought to paint many portraits ...

Letter to Wilhelmina, Auvers-Sur-Oise, May 1890

I think we must not count on Dr Gachet *at all*. First of all, he is sicker than I am, I think, or shall we say just as much, so that's that. Now when one blind man leads another blind man, don't they both fall into the ditch? I don't know what to say. Certainly my last attack, which was terrible, was in a large measure due to the influence of the other patients, and then the prison was crushing me, and old Dr Peyron didn't pay the slightest attention to it, leaving me to vegetate with the rest, all deeply tainted.

Letter to Theo, Auvers, 1890

Church at Auvers
1890

Musée d'Orsay, Paris

Apart from these I have a larger picture of the village church – an effect in which the building appears to be violet-hued against a sky of a simple deep blue colour, pure cobalt; the stained-glass windows appear as ultramarine blotches, the roof is violet and partly orange. In the foregound some green plants in bloom, and sand with the pink glow of sunshine on it. And once again it is nearly the same thing as the studies I did in Nuenen of the old tower and the cemetery, only it is probable that now the colour is more expressive, more sumptuous.

Letter to Theo, Auvers, 1890

Cornfield with Crows
July 1890

Vincent van Gogh Foundation
National Museum Vincent van Gogh, Amsterdam

... There – once back here I set to work again – though the brush almost slipped from my fingers, but knowing exactly what I wanted, I have painted three more big canvases since.

They are a vast field of wheat under troubled skies, and I did not need to go out of my way to express sadness and extreme loneliness. I hope you will see them soon – for I hope to bring them to you in Paris as soon as possible, since I almost think that these canvases will tell you what I cannot say in words, the health and restorative forces that I see in the country.

Letter to Theo, Auvers, 1890

Flowering Almond Blossom
1890

Vincent van Gogh Foundation
National Museum Vincent van Gogh, Amsterdam

... Today I received your good news that you are at last a father, that the most critical time is over for Jo, and finally that the little boy is well. That has done me more good and given me more pleasure than I can put into words. Bravo – and how pleased Mother is going to be. The day before yesterday I received a fairly long and very contented letter from her too. Anyhow, here it is, the thing I have so much desired for such a long time.

No need to tell you that I have often thought of you these days, and it touched me very much that Jo had the kindness to write to me the very night before. She was so brave and calm in her danger, it moved me deeply ...

Well, the result is after all that the child is there – and also that I shall write a letter to Mother telling her so; a day or two ago I started painting a picture for the baby of a blue sky with branches full of blossoms standing out against it. It is possible that I shall send it soon – at least I hope so – toward the end of March. Tomorrow or the day after I shall try to make the trip to Arles again as a kind of trial, in order to see if I can stand the strain of travelling and of ordinary life without a return of the attack.

Letter to Theo, 1890

Self Portrait with Bandaged Ear
1889

Courtauld Institute Galleries, University of London

There are many things I should like to write to you about, but I feel it is useless. ... Since the thing that matters most is going well, why should I say more about things of less importance? My word, before we have a chance to talk business more collectedly, we shall probably have a long way to go ... Well, the truth is, we can only make our pictures speak ... Well, my own work, I am risking my life for it and my reason has half foundered because of it − ... but que veux-tu?

Letter to Theo, Auvers, 1890

CHRONOLOGY

Vincent Willem van Gogh
1853-1890

1853   Born 30 March at Groot-Zundert in Brabant.

1857   Birth of Vincent's brother, Theo.

1869   Vincent given a place at The Hague branch of uncle's firm of art dealers, Goupil and Co.

1873   Sent to London branch of Goupil.

1875   Transferred to Paris branch.

1876   Dismissed from Goupil's.

1877   Works as a bookshop assistant at Dordrecht.
Moves to Amsterdam, planning to read Theology at the University. Eventually decides against this.

1878   Becomes a Bible teacher and preacher to the miners in the impoverished area of the Borinage.

1879   Dismissed by the Brussels director of the mission for his eccentric behaviour.

1880   Writes to Theo that he has decided to take up painting.
Takes lessons in anatomy and perspective in Brussels.

1881 Returns home to Etten. Falls unhappily in love with his cousin, Kee Vos.

1882 Brings his mistress, the prostitute Sien, and her child to live with him in The Hague, despite parental disapproval.

1883 Leaves Sien and goes to Drenthe.

1886 Enters Antwerp Academy, but within the month disagrees with his teachers.
February: Goes to join Theo in Paris. Meets Impressionists and Neo-Impressionists. Arranges exhibition of Japanese prints.

1888 Exhausted by city life, Vincent moves to South of France. Rents a room in the Yellow House, Place Lamartine.
October: Gauguin joins him in Arles.
December: Vincent suffers his first serious mental attack. He cuts off part of his ear and sends it to a prostitute in the local brothel. Gauguin leaves and Vincent is admitted into the mental asylum at St Remy.

1889 Vincent suffers increasingly from intermittent attacks of mental illness. Spends the year in and out of the mental asylum.

1890 Moves to Auvers in northern France under the care of Dr Gachet. Letters to Theo show increasing despair as he becomes more unstable.
July: Goes out into the field and shoots himself. He dies two days later in Theo's arms.
Theo himself dies six months afterwards.

ACKNOWLEDGEMENTS

The editor and publishers would like to thank the following for their help in providing the photographs of paintings reproduced in this book:

Bridgeman Art Library (frontispiece, p77)
Mrs John Hay Whitney (p59)
Musée Rodin, Paris (p31: photo Bruno Jarret)
Photo RMN (pp53, 69, 71)
Photographie Giraudon (p25: Bridgeman-Giraudon, p57: Lauros-Giraudon)
National Gallery of Art, Washington DC (p47)
National Gallery, London (p63)
Rijksmuseum Kröller-Müller, Otterlo (cover, pp13, 15, 29, 33, 35, 37, 61, 67)
Stedelijk Museum, Amsterdam (pp7, 8, 9, 11, 16, 19, 21, 23, 27, 39, 41, 43, 45, 51, 55, 65, 73, 75)
Yale University Art Gallery, New Haven (p49)

We would also like to thank the publisher of the following book for access to the material contained in it which has been reproduced in this volume:

The Complete Letters of Vincent van Gogh Thames & Hudson 1958

Every effort has been made to contact the owners of the copyright of all the information contained in this book, but if, for any reason, any acknowledgements have been omitted, the publishers ask those concerned to contact them.

[80]